This book

belongs to:

_____

Gift Log

Date	From	Gift	Thank You Sent

Gift Log

Date	From	Gift	Thank You Sent

Gift Log

Date	From	Gift	Thank You Sent

Gift Log

Date	From	Gift	Thank You Sent

Gift Log

Date	From	Gift	Thank You Sent

Gift Log

Date	From	Gift	Thank You Sent

Gift Log

Date	From	Gift	Thank You Sent

Gift Log

Date	From	Gift	Thank You Sent

Gift Log

Date	From	Gift	Thank You Sent

Gift Log

Date	From	Gift	Thank You Sent

Gift Log

Date	From	Gift	Thank You Sent

Gift Log

Date	From	Gift	Thank You Sent

Gift Log

Date	From	Gift	Thank You Sent

Gift Log

Date	From	Gift	Thank You Sent

Gift Log

Date	From	Gift	Thank You Sent

Gift Log

Date	From	Gift	Thank You Sent

Gift Log

Date	From	Gift	Thank You Sent

Gift Log

Date	From	Gift	Thank You Sent

Gift Log

Date	From	Gift	Thank You Sent

Gift Log

Date	From	Gift	Thank You Sent

Gift Log

Date	From	Gift	Thank You Sent

Gift Log

Date	From	Gift	Thank You Sent

Gift Log

Date	From	Gift	Thank You Sent

Gift Log

Date	From	Gift	Thank You Sent

Gift Log

Date	From	Gift	Thank You Sent

Gift Log

Date	From	Gift	Thank You Sent

Gift Log

Date	From	Gift	Thank You Sent

Gift Log

Date	From	Gift	Thank You Sent

Gift Log

Date	From	Gift	Thank You Sent

Gift Log

Date	From	Gift	Thank You Sent

Gift Log

Date	From	Gift	Thank You Sent

Gift Log

Date	From	Gift	Thank You Sent

Gift Log

Date	From	Gift	Thank You Sent

Gift Log

Date	From	Gift	Thank You Sent

Gift Log

Date	From	Gift	Thank You Sent

Gift Log

Date	From	Gift	Thank You Sent

Gift Log

Date	From	Gift	Thank You Sent

Gift Log

Date	From	Gift	Thank You Sent

Gift Log

Date	From	Gift	Thank You Sent

Gift Log

Date	From	Gift	Thank You Sent

Gift Log

Date	From	Gift	Thank You Sent

Gift Log

Date	From	Gift	Thank You Sent

Gift Log

Date	From	Gift	Thank You Sent

Gift Log

Date	From	Gift	Thank You Sent

Gift Log

Date	From	Gift	Thank You Sent

Gift Log

Date	From	Gift	Thank You Sent

Gift Log

Date	From	Gift	Thank You Sent

Gift Log

Date	From	Gift	Thank You Sent

Gift Log

Date	From	Gift	Thank You Sent

Gift Log

Date	From	Gift	Thank You Sent

Gift Log

Date	From	Gift	Thank You Sent

Gift Log

Date	From	Gift	Thank You Sent

Gift Log

Date	From	Gift	Thank You Sent

Gift Log

Date	From	Gift	Thank You Sent

Gift Log

Date	From	Gift	Thank You Sent

Gift Log

Date	From	Gift	Thank You Sent

Gift Log

Date	From	Gift	Thank You Sent

Gift Log

Date	From	Gift	Thank You Sent

Gift Log

Date	From	Gift	Thank You Sent

Gift Log

Date	From	Gift	Thank You Sent

Gift Log

Date	From	Gift	Thank You Sent

Gift Log

Date	From	Gift	Thank You Sent

Gift Log

Date	From	Gift	Thank You Sent

Gift Log

Date	From	Gift	Thank You Sent

Gift Log

Date	From	Gift	Thank You Sent

Gift Log

Date	From	Gift	Thank You Sent

Gift Log

Date	From	Gift	Thank You Sent

Gift Log

Date	From	Gift	Thank You Sent

Gift Log

Date	From	Gift	Thank You Sent

Gift Log

Date	From	Gift	Thank You Sent

Gift Log

Date	From	Gift	Thank You Sent

Gift Log

Date	From	Gift	Thank You Sent

Gift Log

Date	From	Gift	Thank You Sent

Gift Log

Date	From	Gift	Thank You Sent

Gift Log

Date	From	Gift	Thank You Sent

Gift Log

Date	From	Gift	Thank You Sent

Gift Log

Date	From	Gift	Thank You Sent

Gift Log

Date	From	Gift	Thank You Sent

Gift Log

Date	From	Gift	Thank You Sent

Gift Log

Date	From	Gift	Thank You Sent

Gift Log

Date	From	Gift	Thank You Sent

Gift Log

Date	From	Gift	Thank You Sent

Gift Log

Date	From	Gift	Thank You Sent

Gift Log

Date	From	Gift	Thank You Sent

Gift Log

Date	From	Gift	Thank You Sent

Gift Log

Date	From	Gift	Thank You Sent

Gift Log

Date	From	Gift	Thank You Sent

Gift Log

Date	From	Gift	Thank You Sent

Gift Log

Date	From	Gift	Thank You Sent

Gift Log

Date	From	Gift	Thank You Sent

Gift Log

Date	From	Gift	Thank You Sent

Gift Log

Date	From	Gift	Thank You Sent

Gift Log

Date	From	Gift	Thank You Sent

Gift Log

Date	From	Gift	Thank You Sent

Gift Log

Date	From	Gift	Thank You Sent

Gift Log

Date	From	Gift	Thank You Sent

Gift Log

Date	From	Gift	Thank You Sent

Gift Log

Date	From	Gift	Thank You Sent

Gift Log

Date	From	Gift	Thank You Sent